Priceless

Priceless

DION PRICE BIOGRAPHY

Story Terrace

Text John Feldman, on behalf of StoryTerrace

Design Grade Design and Adeline Media, London

First print September 2020

StoryTerrace

www.StoryTerrace.com

CONTENTS

FOREWORD

We are hard pressed on every side, but not crushed; perplexed, but not in despair; persecuted, but not abandoned; struck down, but not destroyed.

2 Corinthians 4:8

A native of Bristol, Pennsylvania and one of seven siblings, Dion Eric Price is no stranger to chaos and dysfunction. A victor of small beginnings and a toxic childhood, he navigated the adversities that innately surrounded his youth. He was haunted by feelings of inadequacy and longed for love and support, so he navigated life wearing the mask of rejection and feeling unloved.

After years of living in a toxic household, his mother moved him and three of his siblings to Augusta, Georgia, seeking a better life. They were in a new place, but Dion still struggled with familiar demons. A young man ridiculed for his bad acne, endowed nose and darker skin, he was rocked by hurtful teasing contributing to his suffering from low self-esteem, abandonment, and rejection.

Navigating through life and struggling internally, he turned to using substances. Not wanting to repeat the mistakes of his father and realizing that he needed to make changes in his life, he sought a new path. Dion joined the United States Air Force where he would spend more than twenty years of his life. Traveling the world, meeting people and relishing in new experiences, he had found his niche. However, those same old demons would rear their ugly heads. Married a time or two (or three) Dion repeated the dysfunction he witnessed as a child. With no example of how to navigate manhood, let alone be a good husband, he failed at relationships. Feelings of defeat became a mainstay for him, but, God did not let his story end there... Dion gave his life to Jesus Christ and with God's help, Dion has now turned his Adversity to his Advantage!

With his master's degree in Clinical Mental Health Counseling, he's using his childhood, life experiences and knowledge to make a difference in the lives of others. Dion could have given up, he could have quit on life, but there was something greater brewing in him and it has reached full fermentation. Adversity was just a pothole on the road to Advantage. Sometimes in life, it is the challenges, heartaches and disappointments that show us our worth and I know after you read this book, you will be inspired, encouraged, and motivated. Dion's story is many of our stories. He started his life feeling rejected and at times worthless, but

God showed him his value is more precious than rubies... In other words, he's Priceless!

By:
Trae R. King-Latimer
Command Chief Master Sergeant (ret)
U.S. Air Force

1

THE CRACKED FOUNDATION

Seneca echoed this sentiment when he wrote in his thirteenth letter On Groundless Fears, "We suffer more in imagination than in reality"—words that remind us that people often create their own unnecessary suffering.

1

IT STARTS INSIDE THE HOME

"The reward of suffering is experience."

Experience. This is what we can call our suffering now, after the fact. After it's torn through our lives and done its damage. But at the time, it doesn't seem like experience. At the time, it seems like suffering. It feels like the entire world is pushing down on your shoulders and no matter how loud you yell, no one hears—no matter who you call for, no one comes.

This was how I felt as a child. It was how I felt when I heard my mother's cries every night when my father would hit her. It was how I, myself, also felt when he would hit me. Or one of my siblings. There were so many experiences that I've had throughout my lifetime and they have tried to shape me into a broken person.

But I wouldn't let them. God wouldn't let them. He had a plan for me and although that plan involved a few bumps in the road, it turned out well in the end.

I was born in May of 1968 in Bucks County, Pennsylvania where I lived with both of my parents. They were married at the time, but my father already had three children from his previous marriage and he and my mom would have four more. So there were a total of seven kids living in the house.

Our house was in an old Army barracks. The place had been turned into government housing and it was what we called home for several years. I still remember the blue cinder block walls that would be cold to touch in the winter months. There was no insulation in the walls and the bitter winter cold made its way through. It wasn't the greatest place to live, but we had food on the table and a roof over our head and that's more than a lot of people can say.

Home is a place of comfort and even though mine wasn't as luxurious as I'm sure my parents would have liked, it was a place where we could all be together.

When you think back to your childhood years, where was your place of safety? Was it in your home? With your parents? In the company of loved ones or with friends? Each of us has a different and unique beginning to the story of our lives and although memories of our youngest years seem to disappear as we age, there are some important ones that remain with us as time goes on.

For me, the memory of those blue, cinder block walls is one I will always have. I also have a clear memory of the time we moved out of that house and into Venice Ashby, which was a new neighborhood of government homes that we were able to get into. The homes had just been built and since we had two adults and seven kids in our family, we were able to get into a five-bedroom unit. It was so much bigger than our last home and I remember thinking to myself, We must be rich!

From an outsider's perspective, our family looked as normal as any other. My father had a job and my mother stayed home and tended to the kids during the day. My siblings and I went to school, then came home and played in the neighborhood in the afternoons. We played sports, had our activities, and seemed as happy as can be.

But inside the home was different. Once that door was shut and we were in our own little world, all hell broke loose. And as I grew older, I learned that this is the case for many families—thinking the bad things that went on inside their own home were something that no one else had to deal with. From the outside, all families looked perfect to me. It took me growing up and talking to others to realize this wasn't the case. Only then was I able to realize that I wasn't alone and that these unfortunate situations were more widespread than I could have imagined.

Many of us have secrets that we've held since we were kids. As a child, you don't know what else to do. You don't really know how to process the negative events that occur. For me, negative circumstances of my life began when I was two years old. I don't know what led up to it, but for some particular reason my father hit me with a belt and ended up ripping skin from my navel. The physics of it are still unclear because I never asked for thorough detail, but the belt wrapped around my waist and the buckle got caught onto my midsection as he was pulling it away—the rest is history.

My mother threatened to leave him when it happened. It was one of the many times she would threaten to leave but didn't. When she threatened to leave, he begged her to stay—a common theme between the two during their marriage—and she did. I can only assume her life might have ended up better if she'd left him right then. Regardless, the belt left a scar that still sticks with me to this day.

Many of us have scars, be it physical or emotional. For those who had to grow up with unfortunate circumstances, there are many. And even those who may have grown up being what some would call privileged, there are still scars. This book isn't intended only for those who come from poor, abusive families. Each and every one of us has inner demons. We all have battles in life. We all have bad memories and difficult times fighting through those memories and coming out the other side.

The same held true inside my own childhood household. Not all of my brothers and sisters had the same fate I did. Not all were a victim of my dad's abuse. Dad had his favorites. He'd pick and choose who he wanted to harm and who he wanted to love. When my brother was twelve years old, he tried to run away from home. The result: my dad whipped him with a cable so viscously and so many times that he still has scars on his back to remind him. Yet my sister once broke the glass coffee table and my father simply cleaned the mess for her.

My mother was the unfortunate one who took the abuse on a daily basis. There were seven children in the house so my dad could take out his anger on any of us, which gave the others a break from time to time. But when it came to my mother, there were no other options. My dad had no other wife. He had her, and when he was angry—which was quite often—she was the only one on his radar. The result was never good for my mother. And as much as I remember her crying and pleading, my father never settled down and left her alone. He took advantage of what he could and with children too young to know any better or be able to stand up to him, he continued to do what he'd done within the confines of our home.

While the extent of what took place inside my childhood home isn't too common—or so I truly hope—many families go through negative issues. Fighting. Yelling. Hitting. Neglect and abuse. These are all things children have to deal with and if you're a victim of these circumstances, you know how this affects those who endure it. Witnessing this as a child makes you feel as though it's normal and in turn, it creates an upbringing that will lead to future abuse.

It's easy to think back now, as an adult, and wonder why I didn't say anything. Wonder why my mother never said anything or why my siblings kept quiet. One thing I can tell you is that African American culture doesn't allow for it. In our culture, you suffer in silence. When you go outside your home, you don't say a word about what goes on inside. If you do, then your world inside will end up being worse than it was before you opened your mouth.

At the time this book is written, the National Association of Adult Survivors of Child Abuse reports that 3.3 million children witness domestic violence in their homes each year. So the first thing to note if you are reading this is that you're not alone. There are certainly different levels of domestic abuse, but the fact that this many children are exposed to it means you are not alone.

The problem with this statistic—on top of the eye-opening number—is that it indicates the trend will continue. Children who grow up in abusive homes and find this behavior to be normal will most likely carry out the same behavior in front of their own children.

But this doesn't have to be the case. If you come from an unstable home, you are not destined to go down the same road. You have a choice—a choice to be better. You can change your life. I'm here to tell you from first-hand experience that life can hand you some serious blows and you can witness yourself at ultimate low points, but you can always make a good life for yourself. It just takes a bit more work to do so.

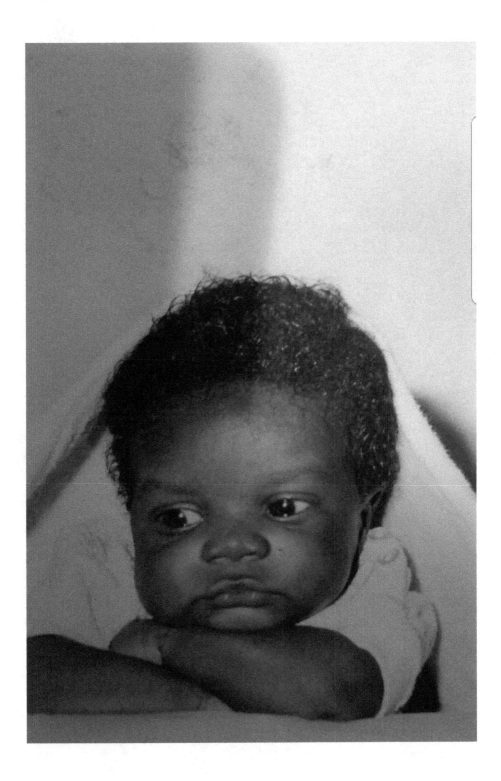

2

EVERYONE NEEDS A MENTOR

I loved playing football as a child. I *loved* it. I had fun playing other games outside with the kids in the neighborhood, but playing football was where I was happiest. I played for the Greater Bristol Yellow Jackets and I carry a lot of memories from those times.

My dad was a big Steelers fan growing up so we all grew up Steelers fans. When I'd watch those games, I'd see John Stallworth out on the field, catching passes and that was who I idolized. I wanted to be a wide receiver when I first started playing, but my coaches put me at running back and that was the position I played throughout my football career. I wasn't the fastest runner when I was out in the open, but man could I make some quick cuts. I felt like Emmitt Smith out there.

I was pretty good. One of the best on the team. Still, I never remember either of my parents coming to watch me play. I could see if I was some third- or fourth-stringer sitting on the bench the whole game, but I wasn't. I was good. I gave them good reason to show up and support me but they never did.

During games, I would hear the crowd roar and look up to see other kids' parents cheering them on. No one ever yelled Dion, though. And that can really weigh on a child. You can begin to wonder if there's something more you can do to get your parents to be as supportive as your teammates'.

I know why my dad didn't come to any games. It was because he was a bad father. He didn't care enough about any of his kids to show that kind of support. My mother, on the other hand, *wasn't* bad. So it surprised me when she never came. It wasn't until later in life that I learned she didn't come because of my dad. Because he wouldn't let her. He didn't let her go anywhere.

My mom didn't have a job. She had seven kids to tend to, but when we were all gone at school for the day, she was home. She had no hobbies and when I was younger, I assumed that was because she had no interest in any. But this was another part of my dad's demands that she not leave the house. When he wasn't home, she wouldn't even leave the porch. She knew his working hours and could have easily gone out during the day without him noticing, but still never went. She had to have been afraid that someone would see her in public and that my dad would find out.

The funny thing is, while she was stuck at home and afraid to leave the house, he was out doing his own thing.

After work, he would go out drinking—a habit of his that was most likely responsible for the way he treated us—and sleeping around. He was a drinker, and adulterer, and an abuser. He was never really there for any of us. The only time he would be was when he wanted to hit us.

For a young boy, a father is supposed to be a mentor. A father is someone you look up to and idolize. Someone you mirror and mimic your actions after. As I would learn later in life, fathers like mine are the reason these abusive traits continue being passed down to future generations. Children absorb so much at a young age and they don't know the difference between right and wrong. They see domestic abuse and think it's normal.

My dad was a steel mill worker and his shift times would vary. Sometimes he would work the first shift from 7:00 a.m. to 3:00 p.m., sometimes he would work the second shift from 3:00 p.m. to 11:00 p.m., and other times he would work the third shift, which was the overnight shift from 11:00 at night until 7:00 in the morning. I always liked it best when he worked the second shift. It meant he would be gone when I got home from school and he wouldn't be back until I was asleep. It meant barely ever seeing him, which also meant he barely saw *me*—and barely had time to hit me.

I hated when he was home and that's not how it should be with a father. I can't speak for all my other siblings, but I know that's how I felt. And I assume it's how my brother felt as well. It had gotten so bad for him that he had an incident when he was a teenager that he'll never be able to forget. Me neither. To this day, I remember him telling me his version of this story and how close all of our lives came to being changed forever.

My dad had a pistol that he kept in the house that he had in the event someone tried to break in. My brother knew where it was and though he never tried to take it or play with it, there was an instance where he couldn't help himself. It was soon after my dad beat him with the cable cord that left him scared that the event took place.

Where we lived, there were fences in front of the homes. They were tall, wooden privacy fences that had staggered planks and you could see out from the inside, but you couldn't see in if you were standing on the outside. One afternoon when my father pulled in front of the house and got out of the car, my brother stood behind the fence, gun in his hand. He watched through the planks as our father walked down the path to the door. My brother followed him with his eyes, looking through the gaps in each plank as he walked, pointing the pistol at him through each one— as my dad walked, the pistol followed. With each plank he walked by, my brother came closer to squeezing the trigger. He wanted to, but he was scared, still only a teenager.

When he finally got the courage, he squeezed hard enough. But all he heard was a click.

My brother pulled the trigger and intended to shoot my dad that day, but the gun jammed. Luckily for my brother, my dad didn't hear the click. He didn't realize what was going on and never found out. I can only imagine the beating that would have taken place if he had.

Somehow, after all the abuse and all the neglect, some of us still sought his approval, and I was one of them. He was always so negative and hateful, yet I wanted him to be happy with me. I even went as far as stealing a gift for him at a church trip, though I ended up getting caught.

On Sundays, my mother and my brothers and sisters would all go to church. This certainly won't be a surprise to you, but my father didn't go. While it was his decision to make the rest of us go, he never went. One year, our church took a trip to Hershey Park for the day and while walking around inside one of the gift shops, I saw this long cigar inside of a wooden case. I knew my dad liked to smoke cigars because I'd seen him smoke them often. As I saw the thing sitting there on the shelf, I thought to myself how much my dad would like it. I could almost see the smile on his face and maybe even feel the embrace of a warm hug he would give me for handing him this gift. The only problem was, I had no money.

I tried to take it from the store without paying and was caught. The church leaders who organized and brought us on the trip were notified and spoke to me about it. But here's the best part: they never said anything to my parents about it. At the time, I was young. I had no idea whether people knew what was going on in my house or whether or not it was normal. But they must have known. They must have been aware of how my dad was with us because they didn't tell him about the incident. They knew he would beat me for it.

How amazing is that? Just thinking of that made me realize that many others must have known about what was going on inside our home. It means I wasn't alone. That we weren't alone. That we might have been able to reach out and start talking to people because they would have been able to talk to us and know exactly what we needed.

What I never realized at the time is how open and willing people might have been to help me, had I reached out. As I have gotten older and spoken to more people, it's surprising how many have gone through tough times and how they wished they would have reached out for help sooner. Communication can be such an effective tool. It can help you to not feel so alone, and that's exactly how I felt for most of my childhood.

But at the time, I was just a kid and I didn't know what options I had. I kept quiet and thanked the Lord that my father didn't find out about me stealing the cigar. Because if he had…well, it would have led to one heck of a whooping.

The people we went to church with were good people. One good thing that came out of our church experience was Reverend Wright, who ended up becoming a good friend of the family—finally, a man in my life who could be a good mentor. And I needed that. I needed a good mentor.

All young people do. We all need someone good and positive in our lives who will help guide us in the right direction to being a decent human being.

3

THE EFFECTS OF
LOW SELF-WORTH

The most important thing to know about having a low self-worth is that you don't get it on your own. It's not something you decide on one day. Having a low self-worth is given to you. It comes from what others say and do. It comes from how loved ones treat you. And when the ones who are supposed to love you the most treat you badly, it's hard to see value in yourself.

This is what happened to my mother. She took a lot of physical and mental abuse from my father, but she wouldn't leave him. She threatened to. Many times. But he always talked her out of it.

Then an incident came that was so bad that she couldn't bring herself to stay with him. It was the last straw. This time, he had gone entirely too far and that gave her the strength to finally leave him. My father might have given her a complex about herself over the years and made her feel invaluable—he made us all feel invaluable—but she put her foot down on this occasion. And we left.

It happened so quickly. Overnight, we were on a bus, leaving Pennsylvania and driving south to Augusta, Georgia to stay with my aunt and uncle—my mom's brother and his wife. When we did, we left behind everything. We left behind friends, school, and I left behind football.

We all made a sacrifice that day, but it *did* lead to one good thing: I didn't have to hear the screams and cries of my mother anymore. Dad wasn't around to hit her, or any of us. But my aunt and uncle would fight just as much as my parents did, and it led to the same result for my aunt. We would hear her cries in the night, but at least it wasn't my mom.

One way to feel better about yourself and gain a bit more confidence is to become independent. This is what my mother did when we got to Augusta. Without my father to rely on financially, she needed to go out and get a job and work for her own money. And she certainly worked hard. She started working at a power plant in Waynesboro, Georgia and worked long hours. She worked those long hours and would come home dirty and sweaty. On top of that, she didn't even have a car, so she had to catch rides with co-workers to and from the plant every day.

My mom used to come in the door and take off her dirty work boots. Then she'd set her hardhat down on the table and sit down to relax. That was when I could see all the sweat. For a woman who hadn't been working—hadn't even left the house—in so many years, this was a completely new life for her. But she was doing it. She went to work every day and did what she had to do for her family.

Every day when she got home, I would sit and talk to her. I would listen to her tell me about how hard work was and how it was draining her.

"I might go back to Freeman," she said. *Freeman. My dad.*

My response when she said this was, "If you go back, he'll kill you." And I truly thought he would.

That amazed me, though. All the bad my father—*Freeman*—had done to her, and she was still thinking about going back to him. It told me one thing: life is *hard*.

She didn't go back to him. My mother was resilient and continued to work hard at the power plant. Eventually she was able to buy a three-bedroom home on her own and we were out of my uncle's house. We didn't have any furniture. Had to rely on Dad saying he would bring some down for us. And he did. He bought some new furniture, but he put that new furniture in his own house and brought his wife and kids the old stuff.

Nice guy.

My mother was an amazing woman. She overcame a horrible situation with my father, moved away, started working, and was able to buy her own home. Proof that you can pick yourself up from any situation, regardless of who is trying to pin you down.

But she wasn't the only one dealing with issues surrounding self-worth at the time. I also felt them. After my mom bought the house, she started working the night shift which meant my siblings and I were home by ourselves at night a lot. We were getting older and entering adulthood and doing all the things teenagers do, including bullying and name-calling. They would call me *puss face* because of my acne. Constantly told me I had a big nose. And definitely gave me a complex about myself.

My mother even chimed in once, asking me, "What happened? You used to have such beautiful skin."

The people I loved most were saying all these bad things to me. Making me feel so low that I wanted to hide in my room and not come out. Or leave the house and not come home. But things outside the house weren't so great either. Since we moved from Pennsylvania to Georgia, I was no longer playing football and didn't have the friendships I had back in Bucks County, Pennsylvania. I didn't even have football to take my mind off of things. Our new high school, Glen Hills, had elementary and middle schools and the kids who were brought up in their school system already had spots on their football team. There was no room for a newcomer, even a good running back like me.

So I had nothing. Couldn't go anywhere. Couldn't talk to anybody. And this was at a time before social media and the internet even existed so I didn't even have those options. I just had me. And that's when I turned to drugs.

So many people resort to these numbing mechanisms when feeling pain and I was admittedly no different. I was given weed to try for the first time when I was ten years old and I didn't look back. My high school years were terrible and I didn't want to be in school, but I had to be. So I started going there drunk. Or high. Or both. I wore the same jacket to school every day and that was my escape. I felt like I could hide inside that jacket.

But I couldn't hide. Low self-worth can't be hidden beneath a jacket because its roots go much deeper.

2

PERCEPTION IS NOT ALWAYS REALITY

Marcus Aurelius clearly felt the same, writing in Meditations: "Very little is needed to make a happy life; it is all within yourself, in your way of thinking." If you can adjust your perspective, you can choose to embrace the positive in life, no matter what it throws at you.

4

DETERMINE YOUR FATE

There are many bad things that can happen in your life, and these things can either make you or break you. Each of us has obstacles in our lives. They come in all forms: health problems, wealth problems, emotional trauma and physical pain.

What's important is that you don't let them define you. That you don't let these issues mold you into something you don't want to be.

When I was a kid, I always wondered why bad things happened to me. And there were *a lot* of bad things that happened to me. The only thing I can say never occurred was that I was never molested. And I'm lucky to say that I wasn't because I've spoken with and befriended people who have, and their life was never the same after.

Although I was in many bad situations, I learned later in life that God put me in those situations for a reason. He was preparing me. There was a purpose behind each negative moment in my life. But as a child, while these things were happening, I could only ask the question of why. *Why had these things happened? What had I done to deserve them?*

As I got older, I began to accept these bad things as reality. To me, they were just part of life. They were happening so often that I began to overlook them. They were normal.

That being said, I didn't want to live my life like that. I didn't want to live around all the negativity, so I began to drink and do drugs. Heavily. Getting drunk and high allowed me to get through my days. I would hide inside that one jacket I wore every single day to school and between that jacket and the drugs and alcohol, I was able to manage. Had I sobered up at any point, I would have subjected myself to the hurtful things I was trying to escape.

I had no friends. I had a bad home life with being made fun of. I had no football. I was one of the few poor kids in a school full of rich kids and didn't fit in with anyone. The only way I got through each day was by being high. And the people in my life knew it. Teachers at school suspected it. One even told me, "I wouldn't be surprised if within one year of graduating, you're either dead or in jail."

It was a horrible thing for her to say, but she wasn't exactly wrong to say it. I mean, I was coming into school high every day. Still, can you imagine an educator today saying something like that to a child? Where's the support? The encouragement?

But this goes to show that you have to determine your own fate. This pessimistic teacher saw me one way, but she had no idea what my home life was like, nor did she take the time to find out. To ask me questions. To see if I was okay.

While in my senior year of high school, I joined the military delayed entry program. And it wasn't to spite that teacher, but to avoid getting a job and staying at my mother's house. My mom had told me that I needed to either get a job once I graduated or move out. I wanted to get away from home anyway. I was constantly being made fun of and up until then, my way of staying out of the house was to hang out with the older people I was getting high with every night.

We all reach for something when we're alone or feeling down. But I felt like I had nothing. No one. Joining the military was going to help me get away from the life I had and, hopefully, start a new one.

The drinking and the drugs didn't stop though. It was bad enough that I was going to school every day high, but when I went to take the Armed Services Vocational Aptitude Battery (ASVAB) high, it was almost inevitable my life was going to continue on a downward roll.

I still passed and I was set to join the Air Force after high school—proof that no matter how bad things can get, you can always take a shot at something new. It was no childhood dream of mine to be in the military, but as the years went on, it was a dream of mine to escape the life I was living. My only choice when I was younger was to get high and forget about the world. But once I got older, I knew I needed something else. I needed a real escape. So I took my shot at something new.

There are going to be moments in your life when things look like they've hit rock bottom. We all have these issues and some have more than others which is to be expected, but that doesn't make you incapable of greater things. Coming from a kid who dealt with abuse and trauma throughout his entire childhood, I can confidently say that this is true.

My life certainly didn't turn around for the better overnight. In fact, it would end up getting worse—much worse. But by joining the Air Force, I was attempting to create a better life for myself. On the day I left for Basic Training, I told my mother that I was never coming back. She wasn't aware of it, but I was leaving a traumatic environment and I wanted to distance myself from it.

Sometimes the people who hurt you don't even realize they're doing so. My brothers and sisters making fun of me would turn out to be an innocent circumstance of kids being kids, but they didn't realize the damage they were doing. What I turned to when this happened was an escape. Had I been open with them and told them how it was affecting me, maybe they would have stopped. Or maybe they wouldn't have. Like I said, they were just kids being kids.

Regardless of how others make you feel, it's so important to know your own value. What others say about you shouldn't define you. The things they say might be hard to ignore or overlook, but if you're able to do so, your life can be so much better. Your fate is determined by your mindset. Don't let the negativity around you drag you down.

5

AFRAID TO FACE THE LIGHT

Having a complex about yourself can significantly hinder your ability to move forward in life. Whether this be from things that happen at home, events in your social life, or any other circumstance that causes you to go into defense mode, having a negative self-image is detrimental to moving on with your life.

Because of my negative self-image, I turned to drinking and drugs.

On the morning on my eighteenth birthday, I was a senior in high school and in the military delayed entry program. Each day that passed was one day closer to me leaving and having the chance to start over. But that didn't change the way I was living my day-to-day life at the time. I was still getting drunk and high every day, and on the morning of my eighteenth birthday, I went a little harder than normal.

I drank a lot before school and even ended up taking some pills. I was in class and my teacher knew I was drunk so she started reprimanding me for being there in the state I was in. She was really letting me have it, first thing in the morning.

And then I threw up on her.

Honestly, I didn't know what to do. I stood there, frozen, and then I remembered one of the kids in the class telling me to run, so I did. I ran out of the school and down to the bottom of the hill where the street was. I don't even remember how I reached out to my friend to come pick me up, but when I got to the bottom of the hill where the street was, I laid down on the sidewalk. The next thing I knew, I woke up in the passenger seat of my friend's car.

I think I can honestly say this was one of the lowest points of my life. And why did it happen? Why was I drinking the way I was? It was because of how I felt about myself. I felt so worthless and so unwanted by everyone in my life that no amount of alcohol was enough.

I went to school the next day. I had no choice. I'd like to say I was embarrassed but I was high so it wasn't as bad as I expected. Early in the day, I was called to the Principal's office and he asked what happened. And he wasn't hiding what he wanted to know. When the Principal spoke to me, he asked if I was drunk or high.

"I just felt sick," I told him.

There was no way I could escape what happened, but I had to lie. At the time, I was one absence away from being held back for the year and if I was held back, it meant I would be kicked out of the delayed entry program for the military.

I had made a decision to better my life yet I couldn't escape the one I was trying to leave behind. I was so close to getting away from it all, but all of my absences—and now this event—led to me being within inches of being kicked out.

The only problem was that it didn't stop me. I wanted so badly to get away from it all, yet I couldn't put down the booze. I couldn't remove myself from the numbness and go back to a life of living with all the self-hate.

For anyone who has ever had problems with addiction, you certainly know the feeling. You want so badly to get away from it all—to rid yourself of the demon. But it has its hands wrapped around you. You have this fear of what life will be like without it. Like you won't be able to function. Like you'll be letting people down. And for me, I couldn't take letting anyone else down. I had a few friends that I drank with and that was it. If I lost them, I'd have nobody.

For me, the high wasn't what I was addicted to. It was the escape from reality.

The day of my real escape came when I left for the Air Force and told my mother I was never coming back home. I was able to escape my life and go through Basic Training. And if you're thinking that I came out the other end of Basic Training a new man, you would unfortunately be wrong.

When I graduated Basic Training, I came out the other side the same man. Worse, actually. For me, things got way worse.

At my first duty station as an Airman, I found a way to get myself into a worse situation with drugs than I had been in during high school. I found myself around people who were smoking crack. And worse, I found myself learning how to cook it.

When someone is as down and out as I was, joining the military couldn't even boost my confidence. And isn't that one of the reasons people join the military? To be able to lift your chin, pull back your shoulders and be proud? There's a ton of pride involved in putting on that uniform and serving your country, but for me, there was nothing. The only thing I was doing was escaping my home life without having to pay for it out of pocket.

I had no self-worth. Felt no sense of pride. And when I ended up getting around people that were cooking and smoking crack, I fell right into the lifestyle.

If there's ever proof that your inner issues can drown you, it's this. On the surface, I was getting my life together by joining the Air Force. Yet inside, I was still struggling, clawing away, trying to find an answer to my problem of why no one could accept me for who I was.

So I went right back to doing what I did in high school: I got high. I hung out and got high all the time and then went into work as if nothing was going on. And I wasn't working for some private company while hiding this habit—I was working for the U.S. military. I knew random drug tests would occur, but it didn't stop me. I kept going, never thinking anything of it. And then one day the random test came and I had no choice but to take it. The following morning, I was called into my commander's office and I told myself this was it. I knew I was being kicked out of the military for drug use. So ironic considering I joined to try to get away from everything I was doing at home.

When I was called into the commander's office, my heart was pounding and I was ready for the worst. I thought I knew what was coming, but it turned out not to be the case. Instead of being caught and discharged from the military, it turned out that my commander had some general news he was sharing with some of the airmen in our company and wanted to inform me. Once he was done relaying the information, I was free to go. Just like that, I could breathe again. No dishonorable discharge. No trip back to Mom's house to face my old life again.

I had gotten so lucky. I was so close to being caught and this should have been a real wakeup call for me. I should have left the drugs behind right then and there. But I didn't. Instead, I went back to my house and celebrated... by getting high.

I would never get better. And the reason is because there was no driving force behind the action. I didn't really want to get better. For those who have struggled with anxiety or depression, you know the feeling. What's the point of getting better? Who can I tell? Who will be happy for me?

Internal doubts can circle around in your head and cause you to wonder if you're even able to do something good like getting sober. And these doubts run through us all—they aren't simply a characteristic of the damaged. But some do have them worse than others. For those who have been subjected to horrible experiences in their lifetime, getting a clear and sober mind might be frightening. You might be afraid of what memories a clear mind could bring back and in that case, it's much harder to want that clear mind.

But you have to confront those demons. What I didn't know at the time this was all happening was that these deep-rooted issues were burning inside me. They needed to get out. I needed to confront them because confronting them was the only way to escape them.

6

FINDING THE DEMON

Before you confront the demon inside you, you have to find it. For some of us, that's easy. For others, it might not be. Some of us may have issues that we never even thought of as demons until others point it out. Maybe that comes in the form of someone informing you that you're standoffish. Or a boyfriend or girlfriend saying you won't open up enough to let them into your life.

There are a million different reasons why someone could have these issues altering their lives. And it's easy for us to pick something we think could be the cause of our problems, yet we know there's a deeper issue. That's normal. Fear comes with digging deep into one's soul to search for issues. But in order to rid yourself of the demon, you have to be willing to bring it to the surface.

For me, finding the demon seemed easy—it was my family. The problem started with my father and it trickled its way down to the life I lived inside my home in Georgia.

All the bad things that I witnessed and all the negative words I heard had all found a place inside me and stayed there.

My dad never put the bottle in my hand or rolled the weed for me, but he certainly was the cause of me turning to those drugs for support. He had done so much to negatively influence my life and I couldn't escape him. I couldn't rid myself of the bad memories and the bad feelings so I got drunk and high. Each time a bad thought would try to make its way to my mind, I would drown it with alcohol. I would shove it back down into the pit of my stomach and leave it there. It was only a matter of time before I would have to face those memories and during one church trip, God gave me that possibility.

Although I was doing bad things with my life, I continued to be a spiritual person. I went to church regularly and went on retreats. On one specific church retreat, all of us were sitting around a fire and the pastor led us in an activity called *Throw it in the fire*. He told each of us sitting around the campfire to get a piece of paper and on that piece of paper, we were to write down one bad memory or person from our lives. We would then toss that piece of paper into the fire and we would be freed from it.

I didn't think much of it at first. I actually couldn't even think of a bad thing to write down. It had been so long since I was around my family and to be honest, I had forgotten all about my dad. I hadn't spoken to him in so long. But after some thought, I remembered. I wrote his name down on that piece of paper, tossed it into the fire, and then I cried like a baby. I can't remember ever crying so hard and it was like the bad things my father did to me and the memories he caused me had left. They came to the surface and brought a wave of sadness I could barely cope with, but then they left. Just like that, gone.

The relief felt great but there was still a level of anger in me. I felt like I shouldn't have had to go through that at all. I was just a kid when all of that stuff happened. Why had my father done this to me? Why had he done that to our family?

I told myself that I wanted to call him. As soon as our fire was done, I walked down to where I could use a phone and I called my dad. I had so many things to say to him. I wanted to make him apologize—I would demand it. I was going to tell him what he'd done to me and how much he affected my life.

But when I called, I didn't have a chance to say any of it. As soon as he answered, he apologized to me. Told me he was sorry for everything. I had spoken to him from time to time before this day and he never once admitted fault for anything he had done. But this time, I didn't even have to say a word. He apologized immediately. And I accepted his apology.

I hadn't been a role model in my adult years to this point and although I was able to find relief in my dad's apology, I still had a lot going on in my own life. I had created my own demons over the years which caused me to make some unwise decisions. One of those decisions was getting married. And I guess you could say there were three bad decisions because I was married three times...and divorced three times.

When each divorce occurred, I looked at my soon-to-be ex-wife and pointed out her flaws and why she was the reason for the marriage ending. But in the end, after looking back on all three relationships, I found that I really needed to look at myself. After all, I was the common denominator. When you're married and divorced three times, you need to take a good, hard look in the mirror. So I did.

My third divorce pushed me to see a counselor and that move transformed my life. I never really had anyone to talk to about the issues going on in my life. The only people I would have had a chance to talk to were my wives, but most of the time they were the issue at hand so I had nobody. Seeing a counselor was one of the best things I've done.

One thing that she opened my eyes to was that it wasn't necessarily my fault that all of my marriages ended. She asked me, "Define what a good marriage is," and the answer I gave her was wrong. To me, a good marriage was a man treating a woman right. I listed basically everything that I didn't see in my own childhood—what I wished my mom could have had in a marriage.

When I said this, my counselor opened my eyes to the fact that I had the wrong idea of a good marriage. The only thing I cared about was giving a woman the life that my own mother didn't have. And that isn't the best way to go about a marriage, as you can see. So the women I married might not have been compatible with me. They were simply women who I liked and who liked me back, and because they liked me back, I wanted to treat them like gold.

Deep down, I really just wanted to see my mother treated like gold. That was an inner-lying issue that stayed with me for a very long time. It was an issue that was never dealt with and in my own mind, I was trying to deal with it by doing for other women what my father never did for my mother.

Demons have many different faces. Not all of them are childhood domestic issues like mine. Where you come from doesn't matter. Your race, religion, gender, or any other physical attribute doesn't matter. Nor do financial status or success. We all have demons inside. We all have things that have gone wrong in our lives and have stuck with us. And we all have issues going on in our lives right now. For most people, a lack of money is their number one problem and they believe the cure is to have that prayer answered and win the lottery. But even then, you will have problems. Rich people have problems just like poor people.

For me, alcoholism was the temporary solution to so many problems. Joining the Air Force wasn't the answer and only introduced me to crack. Even then, the alcohol didn't stop, nor did it even slow down. When I drank, I *really* drank. I drank so much that my body started being able to tolerate so much and I didn't feel normal without it. There was a time where I got a DUI while stationed in Japan and I thought I was going to get kicked out of the Air Force...again.

I was pulled over after having one beer and one shot at a friend's barbecue. I rolled through a stop sign and was pulled over.

"Have you been drinking?" the military policeman, or MP, asked me.

"I had one beer at a friend's house," I said, which was true.

"Okay," the MP said. "Would you mind stepping out and taking a field sobriety test for me?"

"Sure." I did. And I passed. But the MP still seemed skeptical so he gave me a breathalyzer test and that's where he discovered that my blood alcohol content was nearly three times the legal limit. Had a normal person had the amount of alcohol in their body, it might have killed them. But I was just fine, functioning and going about my day. Had it not been for the luck of an old commander I worked under putting in a good word for me—because even though I was a drinker, I still worked hard and was damn good at my job—my military career could have ended that day.

It wasn't until I was back home in the year 2000 that I was finally able to beat this habit. I remember vividly, being at church with a new girlfriend of mine on New Year's Eve. I was drunk, listening to the pastor and everything he said was sticking with me. And something that night clicked. I went home and poured out all the liquor in my house and prayed that God would take the taste of liquor out of my mouth.

And he did. To this day, I haven't once been drunk.

3

YOUR ADVERSITY IS
YOUR ADVANTAGE

Challenge is an inevitable part of life, yet when put it into perspective, those challenges help you to grow as a person. And another beautiful benefit of going through hard times is that you can pass all those inevitable lessons on to others!

7

NOT EVERYTHING IS AS IT SEEMS

Looking at the world through your own eyes all the time is tough. What I mean by this is that there are different vantage points. Not everyone sees what you see. They don't focus on the same things you focus on.

Think about how many times you've been out in public and heard someone around you laugh. Are they laughing at you? Did you do something wrong? This is the simplest and most common way of realizing that things aren't always what they seem.

When I was in high school, I wore a jacket every single day because I wanted to hide inside it. My brothers and sisters made fun of my skin and my nose and I felt so worthless whenever in public. My assumption was that everyone who looked at me saw what my siblings saw. I thought I was ugly. I had no confidence whatsoever. As a kid, I don't think I ever talked to a girl when I was sober—one of the reasons I got drunk and high every day. I went out and hung at other people's houses and they were always older, so they were the only people I really spoke with. My first sexual encounter wasn't even something special that I shared with a girl my own age. My first experience was with a married woman at one of these houses I would hang out in every night.

Without any confidence, I never spoke to girls at my school. In my mind, they were all looking at me and calling me *puss face* and *big nose* just like my brothers and sisters were doing at home. I went about my days and graduated, not really talking to anyone. After graduation, all the other seniors were going out to parties, but I went home. I'd been doing plenty of late-night hanging out and getting high and drunk during my high school years so it wasn't the partying that I was missing, it was the lack of any friends that hurt.

My own stance on the matter was that I was ugly and no one would want to talk to me. Especially not any girls. And it took until around 1995 to be proven wrong.

When I was on assignment in Turkey in 1995, I used some of my leave time to go on a trip to Germany with the Masonic Fraternity. While there, I ran into someone who made me realize just how small of a world we live in. I was talking to one of my brothers in the fraternity one day and mentioned my high school, Glen Hills High School. "No way," he said. And then he said a girl's name to me and asked me if I knew her.

"Oh yeah, I remember her!"

"That's my wife. I'll have to bring her around so you can say hi."

The truth was I knew *of* her—I didn't really *know* her. I didn't really know anyone in my high school and hadn't talked to anyone from the school since the day I graduated and went home instead of going out and partying.

My fraternity brother brought his wife around one day, as promised, and I got the chance to talk to her. We reminisced about some things and then it somehow came up that she and all the other popular girls at Glen Hills thought I was cute and wanted to talk to me, but I was too quiet and never said anything.

Can you believe that?

All those years of hiding in my jacket. Of being antisocial because I felt so worthless and ugly. All of it for nothing because, as it turns out, they thought I was cute. I could only think at that very moment of how much better my high school days could have been if I would have known this.

It turned out that the only people who were talking badly about me were the members of my family. Outside of my home, people thought differently. The girls at my school thought I was cute. They had a different vantage point. They didn't hear anyone call me *puss face* or *big nose* or any other name so they never thought of it themselves.

Perspective is everything. The girls at my school thought I was good-looking just the way the Air Force thought I was an innocent person behind closed doors. I was good at my job and would get put into leadership positions as a result. I was in charge of telling others how to act and what to do with their lives, yet I couldn't even control my own. Behind closed doors, I was a mess. I was drinking, sleeping around, and doing everything a good military leader shouldn't be doing.

These two points in my life taught me that everything is certainly not as it seems. And this is incredibly important to realize today, as social media plays an impactful part of our lives. When you look at the smiling faces of others as they post, telling you about the good times being had and great moments in their life, know that this isn't an everyday occurrence. No one can live a life like that. It isn't possible.

You should never look at someone else's life and compare it to yours. That's a recipe for disaster. It can lead to some serious self-doubt and create an overall negative mindset.

The same mindset should be held for those around you, too. Try not to judge others for how they act or where they are in life. That homeless person begging for your change? It's easy to assume that they're lazy or unwilling to do better for themselves, but you honestly have no idea what they've been through. There are people around us that we always view as different than us, but nobody has been given the same life we've been given. We are all God's children and He has given us our own, unique path.

Feelings of self-doubt and worthlessness can enter your mind quickly if you allow them to. But if you go through life with an optimistic and confident mindset, these negative feelings are pushed from your thoughts.

The perception of what others think is simply that: a perception. Don't let the idea of what others might be thinking alter your life. Have confidence in everything you do and you will live a much happier life.

8

OVERCOME THE ODDS

While having confidence in everything you do can help to create a more positive way of thinking, it unfortunately cannot remove the roadblocks that are bound to appear in your life. Issues will always arise. Bad things will happen. But if you find ways to get past all the bad and overcome the odds stacked against you, you will develop a much greater sense of self-worth and confidence.

When my high school teacher at Glen Hills told me I'd either be dead or in jail within a year of graduating, I didn't doubt her. Although my grades were never bad, I didn't do anything but the bare minimum. I came to school—though I missed often—did what I was told and went home. I didn't study, seek help, or even communicate with my teachers. I really just didn't care about school. At all.

I was a drinker and a drug user while in high school. I was a mess. And my teacher had every right to question me, though her approach was pretty forward and not very empathetic. During my high school years and my first few years in the Air Force, nothing changed. That was mainly because I didn't have anyone or anything I cared about enough to stop.

And then my first daughter was born.

On the day my daughter was born, I quit drugs cold turkey. I held my daughter in my arms and told myself I had to stop. I needed to be there for her. This was a scenario that played out in my head for so many years: being a father and holding my child. I always told myself that I would never be like my father was with me. I was going to be there for my kids. I would go watch them play sports. Hug them instead of hit them. Teach them how to be good people. And always be around when they needed me. If I would have continued doing drugs, I wouldn't have been able to do all of those things. I feared I would go right down the same path as my own father.

To this day, people hear that I quit drugs cold turkey and they ask me if I went through withdrawal. They ask about having sweats or night terrors and whatever else is associated with quitting a drug addiction cold turkey, and I tell them all the same thing: I had none. I didn't have any negative effects, but there might have been a reason for that: my drinking intensified. So while I wasn't doing drugs, I was still drinking enough to stay high.

Having a daughter scared me, but I was doing what I could to be a better father. I wasn't in a relationship with her mother so I didn't have my daughter all the time, which was my excuse for being able to drink so consistently. But I did get a girlfriend shortly after and ended up marrying her and having two more kids. All of a sudden, I was 23 years old with three kids and panicking.

I was about to find out if I could be a better father to my kids than my dad was to me. I was drinking just like my dad did, but what I didn't have was the urge or temptation to hit my kids. I never wanted to hurt them. When they got into trouble, I would discipline them, but never even came close to the extent my father took it. I never had the urge to hurt them. Never felt pleasure in having to discipline them. I only did what I had to do to make sure my children understood that they were being punished when they needed to be. And to this day, I still have a healthy and loving relationship with all of my kids.

Each time my kids got into some sort of trouble, I always thought back to my own childhood. I remembered how much I dreaded beatings and there was one particular incident that continues to stand out—one that was an accident but gave me one of the worst beatings.

When I was in grade school, I was playing at recess with another boy and we were throwing a Nerf football back and forth. If you're not familiar, Nerf footballs are basically made of foam. Their entire brand is made of toys that are safe and prevent kids from getting hurt.

The kid I was having a catch with was a white kid, and he

was really white. His skin was fair and that would turn out to be bad for me because one pass I threw hit him right in the face. Since we were playing with a Nerf football, it should have been fine. But his nose started to bleed and he cried and to make matters worse, his mother was on the school board. She found out and called my mother who then had to come pick me up from school.

It was a simple mistake, but since the kid I was playing with was so fair and his skin bruised easily, it looked much worse. My mom took me home and beat me so badly that I was crying for my dad to help me. If you've been following along with me throughout this book, you know that it would take a whole lot for me to want my dad.

Even if he was home, it wouldn't have helped. He probably would have joined in. I know this because I remember the smile that came across his face when he got home from work that day and my mom told him about what happened and how she punished me. That smile was sick and twisted. I can still see it. And I never wanted to be like that. I never wanted my kids to think I took pleasure in disciplining them.

As bad as that story makes both of my parents seem, they actually had odds against them, too. What I've learned is that you shouldn't judge someone from what you see on the surface because there's so much more to it. Each one of my parents had demons of their own that they were dealing with and they were trying to live a normal life while doing so.

My mother's parents died when she was young and she was sent off to live with her aunt and uncle. But they still mistreated her. Although she was family, she was never shown any sort of affection or love. So for her to show us any kind of love was a big deal for her. In her mind, she was much better than the family who took care of her as a child.

As for my dad, he was one of twelve children and when he was still in school, his mother left them. So he and his brothers had to drop out of school and work at the local mill to provide for the rest of the children. He was able to provide and that was all he did. Providing was all he knew and he was never shown any affection. He never had a loving mother to be there to hold him when things went wrong. He never even really had a childhood. The only way he ever knew how to show love was by working to put food on the table and shelter over the heads of the ones he cared about.

We can't expect our parents to give us something that they never had. If you're reading this and can relate to abuse or neglect from your parents, there may be a reason. Try to find out what their life was like growing up and see where the problems lie.

My parents were given certain sets of information regarding how to be parents and that information was flawed. I don't think either of my parents can be blamed for their actions. They did the best they could with the tools they were given.

9

BECOME PRICELESS

The term *priceless* is defined as "having a value beyond all price; invaluable." It's the way I finally feel about myself and the way each and every one of us should feel. No matter how you feel others view you or how difficult it may be to find self-love and self-confidence, we must all know that we have it within us. We all have traits that define us and separate us from the rest. These are the things that make us unique—the things that make us *priceless*.

I have been blessed with the life I was given. It may not sound that way from the stories you've heard in this book, but these unfortunate circumstances were all part of God's plan for me. He had me go through these events so that I could help. So that I could know from first-hand experience how to help people who are in similar situations.

It's crazy to think that it's so possible to pull yourself out of a tough time. Notice I didn't say the word easy, because it certainly won't be. For those of us who have to overcome so much in our lives, the process is not simple. It's hard. Grueling. Most times it will feel like pushing a rock up a hill but once you get to the top, it's all worth it.

In my lifetime, I have talked to so many people who have had issues they've struggled with, or *are struggling* with. And I take comfort in the fact that there are so many of us who have problems in our lives. It means that the perfect, smiling picture being posted online is just a smokescreen for what's going on in our everyday lives. It's nice to be able to talk to people and hear them tell *real* stories of pain and despair and it's not because I like hearing about it, but because I enjoy being able to watch the relief come out with their words. So many of us hold these negative feelings and emotions inside of us because we feel as though no one else has issues. That ours are rare and therefore not warranted as things that can be resolved.

There are two people who have helped me to really break through the barrier of being a broken person to becoming whole, and they are God and my counselor. God put me through some tough situations and didn't help me because He knew that I would figure things out on my own, and that I would one day use those experiences to help many others. And my counselor helped me because she was able to dig deep and find the root of my issues. She made it possible for me to stop pointing the finger at myself for everything that happened. She gave me something I hadn't had since my younger years when I was running around on the football field with the Greater Bristol Yellow Jackets. She gave me self-confidence.

My counselor inspired me. She opened up my eyes to an entirely new version of me that I could be happy with. One that I could be proud of. No more *puss face* or *big nose*. I was Dion Price. I had four beautiful kids of my own as well as the privilege of being able to help raise several stepchildren. On top of that, I had retired from a long career in the Air Force and I was ready to go out and help others. I was ready to make an impact with my life instead of simply drinking it away.

With my newfound confidence, I went back to school to get my bachelor's degree in Religion and started pastoring at my church. I was helping people in a way I never thought possible and it felt so good to be able to do so. I was so happy with helping that I went back to school and got my master's degree in Theology. After that, I opened a mentorship business where I helped to mentor others and guide them down a right path in life. I also became a life coach, a Christian counselor, and a member of the National Society of Leadership Success.

The pride was pouring out of me now because I felt like I was making a real difference in the world. The kid who used to hide in his jacket and get high to block out the world was now doing things to help others. I began a motivational speaking career and a subsequent company called *Becoming Priceless* where, to this day, I've been happy to share my unfortunate life stories in hope of helping others who feel helpless and lost.

Everything was going great and I didn't want to stop. I wanted to keep going and to get better at helping others so I went to school again and got my master's degree in Clinical Mental Health Counseling where I graduated Chi Sigma Iota and finished within the top 5% of my class. I already knew how to help people, but with this degree I was able to learn the language of a counselor and to really dive deeper into the clinical aspects of helping people recover.

At the same time I was doing this, I started losing a lot of weight, exercising, and eating healthier. I was completely transforming my life for the better and it felt great. It felt like I had become victorious against my own mindset. Like I was in a battle with myself and came out a better person.

What I've learned through all of my experiences is if the foundation of your life is dysfunctional, your entire life will be. You can think of this like a house. When building a house, the foundation is what supports everything else. If there's a crack in the foundation, that's a big problem. The entire house could come crumbling down at any moment.

Dysfunction is dysfunction. It doesn't have gender, race, religion, or social status. It can impact anyone. And the key to beating it is to find the root cause. As mine was able to do for me, a counselor can help you get to the root of your problem. They can help you to solve the maze in your mind of how you got to where you are and why these underlying issues can't seem to go away.

If you're having issues and trying to find the cause of your problems—or simply need someone to talk to—I would highly recommend seeing a counselor. You can also pray to God and ask Him why these things are happening to you. He may answer you or He may leave you to find out on your own, which is what He did for me. He knew I would stumble upon the path I should be on and I did.

Asking for help is not a weakness. It's a strength. Asking for help means you are smart enough and confident enough to know that you need someone or something else. It also means that you are willing and ready to better yourself and to become an asset to the world, not a liability. Or better yet, it means you are ready to do the following:

Be a victor, not a victim.

Story Terrace